4

Ingredients

Gluten Free
Lactose Free

Kim
McCosker

4
Ingredients
Gluten Free
Lactose Free

4 Ingredients
PO Box 400
Caloundra QLD 4551

ABN: 17 435 679 521

FB: facebook.com/4ingredientspage
YT: 4 Ingredients Channel
W: 4ingredients.com.au
TW: @4ingredients

4 Ingredients Gluten Free Lactose Free

Photography:	Angie Simms, www.simmsquinn.com
Cover & Formatting:	Splitting Image
	www.splittingimage.com.au
Printing & Binding:	Leo Paper Group
Australia Publisher:	Simon & Schuster
New Zealand Publisher:	Random House
UK Publisher:	Simon & Schuster
USA Publisher:	Atria Books (a division of Simon & Schuster, USA)
ISBN:	978-0-9806294-6-0

4 Ingredients Wellness Trilogy

I enjoy people. I love to engage with, talk with and listen to people. By nature I ask many questions, as my greatest learnings come from everyday, busy people – just like me. And it's often where the best ideas for future books and projects stem from – people just like you.

This is exactly how the *Wellness Trilogy* came to be. From conversations on our Facebook page, emails to info@4ingredients.com.au and your interest at my public engagements, the most frequently asked questions are; when are you bringing out a *4 Ingredients* book relating to Gluten, Lactose, Diabetes and Allergies? So for you all … *Here they are!*

Three beautiful, affordable books each with over 60 quick, easy and delicious recipes aimed to encourage us all; not only to eat better, but to prevent … *Prevention is the best Medicine!*

Watch for *Wellness Tips* **WT** throughout the trilogy.

Welcome to My Kitchen

I speak all over the world, sharing my story and love
for all things *super-simple* in the kitchen.

I start by saying 'Welcome to my kitchen.'
It's full of love and laughter, of creative simplicity,
recipes and kitchen wisdom that *will* save you time
and money in the kitchen …
It's EASY!

With Love
Kim

What is Gluten?

Gluten is a protein found in wheat, rye, barley, oats and their derivatives. It is also found in grains that are genetic variants, such as spelt and kamut..

Coeliac Disease is an autoimmune reaction, which causes inflammation and damage to the small intestine when gluten is ingested. Those with coeliac disease are intolerant of gluten lifelong, where the only method of treatment is a strict gluten free diet. The exposure of small amounts of gluten to the small intestine will trigger the immune system, resulting in the small intestine lining to become damaged and inflamed reducing the ability to absorb nutrients from the diet.

Non-coeliac gluten intolerance can occur in those that experience the same symtoms as coeliac disease, but test to have no intestinal damage.

Symptoms. This leads sufferers to experience symptoms of malabsorption, including;

- *chronic fatigue*
- *neurological disorders*
- *nutrient deficiencies*
- *anemia*
- *nausea*
- *bloating*
- *skin rashes*
- *depression, and more.*

Research suggests* that 1 in 100 Caucasian's are diagnosed with coeliac disease and 1 in 20 with a non-coeliac gluten intolerance. However, experts suggest that the true number could be closer to 1 in 5 but *many go undiagnosed* living with the symptoms of bloating, abdominal discomfort, pain or diarrhea and headaches, thinking that it's just *'life!'*

For more information and support contact:

Australia   www.coeliac.org.au   1300 458 836
New Zealand   www.coeliac.org.nz   09 820 5157

*Cattassi. C. et al. When is a coeliac a coeliac? Report of a working group
of the United European Gastroenterology week in Amsterdam.

Coeliac
Australia

What is Lactose?

Lactose is the sugar found in milk and dairy products.

Lactase is an enzyme produced by the small intestine that breaks down lactose so that it can be absorbed into the bloodstream.

Lactose Intolerance is caused by the inability of the body to break down milk sugar (lactose). People with this condition cannot produce enough lactase to breakdown the lactose.

What happens? When lactose moves through the large intestine *(or colon)* without being properly digested, the undigested lactose absorbs water and is fermented by natural gut bacteria to produce excessive gas causing uncomfortable symptoms (listed below). Some people who have lactose intolerance cannot digest any lactose containing milk or dairy products at all. Others can eat or drink small amounts of milk products or certain types of milk products without problems.

Lactose intolerance most commonly **runs in families**, and symptoms can occur at any stage in the life cycle.

Symptoms usually begin 30 minutes to 2 hours after you eat or drink milk products. If you have lactose intolerance, your symptoms may include:

- *Bloating*
- *Pain or cramps*
- *Gurgling or rumbling sounds in your belly*

- *Gas*
- *Loose stools or diarrhea*
- *Vomiting*

If you suspect this may be you, always consult your GP or physician first, as there may be alternative conditions causing your symptoms.

Guide to Weights and Measures

GF LF = Gluten Free Lactose Free

To help a recipe turn out right, you need to measure right. I have included this simple conversion table to help, regardless of where you are in the world.

Grams – pounds & ounces

Grams (g)	Ounces (oz.)	Grams (g)	Ounces (oz.)
5g	¼ oz.	225g	9 oz.
10g	½ oz.	250g	10 oz.
25g	1 oz.	275g	11 oz.
50g	2 oz.	300g	12 oz.
75g	3 oz.	325g	13 oz.
100g	4 oz.	350g	14 oz.
125g	5 oz.	375g	15 oz.
150g	6 oz.	400g	1 pound (lb.)
175g	7 oz.	700g	1½ lb.
200g	8 oz.	900g	2 lb.

Spoons – millilitres (mls)

1 teaspoon	5 mls
1 dessertspoon	10 mls
1 tablespoon	15 mls

Cups – mls – fluid ounces – tbsp.

Cups	Mls	Fluid Ounces	Tbsp.
⅛ cup	30 ml	1 fl oz.	2
¼ cup	60 ml	2 fl oz.	4
⅓ cup	80 ml	2.5 fl oz.	5.5
½ cup	125 ml	4 fl oz.	8
⅔ cup	160 ml	5 fl oz.	10.5
¾ cup	190 ml	6 fl oz.	12
1 cup	250 ml	8 fl oz.	16

Table of Contents

Breakfast

Water is the most important nutrient in our diet
And often the most neglected!

Almond Milk

Serves 4

- *1½ cups (220g) raw almonds*
- *4 cups (1 litre) water*

Into a large bowl, place the almonds then the water. Soak overnight to soften, then drain. Blend the almonds with 4 cups of water. Using a very fine strainer or sieve, or several layers of muslin, drain the 'milk' into a large bowl. Squeeze or press the remaining pulp to remove the last of the liquid. The almond meal leftover can be dried or frozen and used to add more fibre to your diet. Refrigerate the milk for 4 to 7 days, covered. It will usually need shaking before serving, to remix.

(WT) *I make this recipe in my Thermochef, simply blend 1 minute / speed 10. For a slightly thicker milk, use 250g almonds and 900ml water.*

Avocado Fan

Serves 2

- *½ cup hummus*
- *½ avocado*
- *2 poached eggs*
- *1 teaspoon fresh dill*

Place 2 tablespoons of hummus onto 2 plates. Peel the avocado, and slice lengthways. With the palm of your hand, gently spread the slices apart to fan. Take half and place on the hummus. Then top each with a poached egg. Season to taste and serve with a smattering of fresh dill.

WT *Poaching eggs is one of the easiest, quickest and lowest calorie ways of preparing eggs, as there is no added fat. When poaching eggs, fill a deep saucepan half with water and bring to a rapid boil. Crack an egg into the water and with a spoon whirlpool the water around the egg to create an even oval shape. Allow to cook until the whites become firm and the yolk is soft to the touch, 2 to 3 minutes.*

Blueberry Pancakes

Makes 6

- *1 cup GF self raising flour*
- *1 cup almond milk*
- *1 egg*
- *½ cup fresh blueberries (extra for serving)*

In a bowl, whisk together the flour, milk and egg. Add the blueberries and mix well. In a large nonstick frying pan over medium heat, drop a quarter cup of the batter into the pan. Make two or three pancakes at a time. Cook for 3 minutes or until small bubbles appear on the surface, then turn and cook another 2 to 3 minutes or until golden. Cover with kitchen paper to keep warm. Repeat with remaining batter. Serve with a dollop of GF LF yoghurt (optional) and the rest of the blueberries.

(WT) *Blueberries are colloquially known as 'Brain-berries.' They are very low in calories – 100g fresh berries provides only 57 calories – and they possess many health benefits. They are high in soluble dietary fibre, minerals, vitamins, and are among the highest anti-oxidant fruits around. All this, means that they contribute immensely towards optimum health and wellness.*

Egg White Omelette

This is a great way to start the day. Customizable and packed with protein, add whatever chopped veggies and herbs you have to make this your own.

Makes 2

- *4 egg whites*
- *2 tablespoons chopped fresh herbs*
- *2 teaspoons garlic-flavoured olive oil*
- *½ cup freshly shaved Parmesan cheese*

In a medium bowl, combine the egg whites, herbs, 1 teaspoon water, season with sea salt and cracked pepper and whisk until frothy. In a 20cm nonstick frying pan, heat one teaspoon of the oil over medium heat. Add half of the egg mixture, swirling to evenly coat the base of the pan. Cook over medium heat until almost set, about 2 minutes. Add half the Parmesan cheese. Using an egg-flip, lift half the omelette over itself and let cook for another 1 to 2 minutes or until completely set. Remove and repeat with the remaining ingredients. Serve sprinkled with a few shavings of Parmesan cheese and/or fresh herbs.

(WT) *Parmigiano Reggiano (Parmesan cheese made in certain regions of Italy) cheese is 100% lactose free. The reason is that within 6 to 8 hours after the cheese is made, lactose is transformed into easy-to-digest lactic acid through the action of enzymes in the cheese. Knowing that Parmigiano Reggiano is naturally lactose free is important—not only is it loaded with calcium but each serving supplies other nutrients such as protein, vitamins and minerals.*

For more interesting information see: www.parmesan.com/health/lactose-free-cheese/

Iced Coffee

To make the coffee cubes, simply make a cup of coffee then pour it into an ice cube tray and freeze.

Makes 2

- *1 teaspoon raw honey*
- *2 cups coconut milk*
- *2 scoops GF LF vanilla ice cream*
- *4 or 6 coffee ice cubes*

In a blender, combine the honey, coconut milk and ice cream, then mix. Pour into two tall glasses, adding 2 or 3 coffee ice cubes to each, makes these icy cold, creamy and sweet.

(WT) *Coconuts are thought by some to be a miracle food, helping to protect and cure the body of internal and external ailments. Coconut milk has many uses, most of which build up the immune system and the body's defences … In summary, drink more coconut milk!*

Peanut 'Better'

Makes 1 jar

- *200g peanuts*
- *50g macadamia nuts*

In a food processor, combine the nuts and blend until nice and smooth. Stop to scrape down the sides, pushing the mixture onto the blades and blend to the desired consistency. Store in an airtight jar for up to 1 month.

WT *Peanuts contain monounsaturated fat (the heart-healthy kind), as well as vitamin E, niacin, folate and fibre. Use a tablespoon in your soups and smoothies; spread over apple, pear and bananas; or use in the sensational* **Peanut Butter Cookies** *(page 38). Or make this tasty* **Satay Sauce**: *Combine ½ cup peanut butter, ½ cup coconut milk, ¼ cup water, 2 tablespoons GF sweet chilli sauce, and 1 to 2 teaspoons curry powder—FABULOUS!*

Quinoa Porridge

Serves 2

- *2 cups almond milk*
- *1 cup quinoa, rinsed*
- *2 tablespoons honey or agave nectar*
- *1 cup fresh blueberries, plus more for serving*

In a small saucepan, bring the milk to a gentle boil. Add the quinoa and return to a boil. Reduce the heat to low and simmer, covered, until three-quarters of the milk has been absorbed, about 15 minutes. Stir in the honey or agave nectar. Cook, covered, until almost all the milk has been absorbed, about 8 minutes. Add the blueberries, stir, and cook for 30 seconds. Serve with additional milk, if required, and sprinkle with blueberries.

WT *Quinoa (pronounced keen-wah) is not a grain; it is actually a seed and is related to the spinach family. Quinoa as a vegetable source of protein contains the right proportion of the 9 essential amino acids, to support the biological function of the human body.*

There is beauty in everything
around us if we take the time to see it
(even in wild growing weeds)

Tropical Breakfast Risotto

Serves 4

- *1 cup (185g) Arborio rice*
- *1 can (400ml) coconut milk*
- *¼ cup organic raisins*
- *1 cup chopped, firm banana*

In a medium saucepan, combine 2 cups of water with the rice and bring to a boil. Reduce the heat to medium-low and simmer uncovered, stirring frequently for creaminess. When the water has been absorbed, add the coconut milk. As that gets absorbed, but while still creamy, fold through the raisins and banana. Heat for another 2 to 3 minutes and serve while the rice is warm and tender.

WT *This is lovely with a variety of tropical fruits—papaya, mango, passionfruit, or pineapple—and sprinkled with some toasted, flaked almonds for a crunchy finish. This dish should be creamy and moist; if too thick, stir in a little more water before adding raisins and bananas. Coconut milk is an excellent substitute for cow's milk because it is easy to digest, simple to make and contains an abundance of nutrients … Drink it plain, use it for cooking, or blend it with smoothies to benefit from its nutritional value.*

Snacks

Almond Butter & Banana Fudge

Makes 12 squares

- *½ cup coconut oil*
- *½ cup almond butter*
- *¼ cup raw honey*
- *½ mashed banana*

Place all the ingredients in a blender and blend until smooth. Pour the mixture into a 9cm square dish lined with baking paper. Allow the mixture to cool in the fridge for at least 2 hours. Slice into 2cm squares and serve immediately.

WT *For an equally yummy* **Maple Walnut Fudge***: Substitute pure maple syrup for the honey. Blend until smooth and fold in ½ cup chopped walnuts. Because of the coconut oil, these types of fudges will melt if not kept in the fridge or freezer.*

Date Loaf

Absolutely blissful!

Serves 10

- *2 teaspoons instant coffee*
- *375g packet dates, chopped*
- *1 cup (175g) GF self raising flour*
- *1 punnet of raspberries*

Preheat oven to 180°C. Add the instant coffee to 1 cup (250ml) of boiling water and stir well. Into a bowl, pour the coffee over the dates and soak overnight. Stir in the flour. Spoon the mixture into a paper lined 20cm springform cake pan, and bake for 45 minutes. Remove and cool, when ready to serve pile high with fresh, seasonal raspberries.

(WT) *Substitute flaked almonds for raspberries, but sprinkle them over the batter before baking for a nice crunchy texture and taste.*

Energy Bars

Makes 12

- *1 cup (120g) dates*
- *¾ cup (200g) crunchy peanut butter*
- *½ cup (60g) shredded coconut*
- *3 tablespoons raw cocoa powder*

Place all the ingredients into a food processor or blender and blend until well combined. Spoon the mixture into a paper-lined 20 x 10cm loaf tin. Smooth the top with the spatula (or back of a spoon). Refrigerate for at least 1 hour. Cut into bars. Keep in the refrigerator in an airtight container.

WT *To make your own peanut butter see **Peanut 'Better'**, page 22.*

Mandarin Friands

Makes 12

- *2 large mandarins, peeled and seeded*
- *1½ cups almond meal*
- *3 eggs, separated*
- *2½ tablespoons agave nectar*

Preheat the oven to 180°C. In a food processor, combine the mandarins, almond meal, egg yolks, and agave and blend for 10 seconds. Whisk the egg whites in a clean, dry bowl until soft peaks form, about 4 minutes. Gently fold the mandarin mix into the egg whites. Divide among 12 nonstick muffin or friand moulds and bake for 20 minutes.

WT *Like all other citrus fruits, mandarins are characterized by their high vitamin C content. Just 2 mandarins a day satisfies the recommended daily intake (RDI) of vitamin C. Note: Men and pregnant women need 40mg/day, women and children need 30mg/day.*

Peanut Butter Cookies

This is a recipe from my very first book, 4 Ingredients, published in March 2007. Since then, my guess is that I have made over 2,000 of these cookies ~ they are good!

Makes 20

- *1 cup crunchy peanut butter*
- *1 cup firmly packed brown sugar*
- *1 tablespoon ground cinnamon*
- *1 egg*

Preheat the oven to 180°C. Line 2 baking trays with baking paper. In a bowl, mix together all the ingredients. Using a tablespoon, roll into balls then place on the baking tray. Slightly flatten with fork tines. Bake until a thin crust forms on the cookie, 8 to 10 minutes. Let cool completely. Store in an airtight container.

(WT) *Peanuts pack a serious nutritional punch and offer a variety of health benefits. Just a handful of raw peanuts per day provides enough recommended levels of antioxidants, minerals, vitamins, protein and are an excellent source of omega 9. Although omega 9 can be produced by the body they are also important from the diet. The main function of omega 9 is that is helps to produce the good cholesterol (HDL) which in turns helps to reduce the bad cholesterol (LDL).*

Tamari-Nuts & Seeds

I love the all round joyous reception every time I serve these … delicious!

Serves 4

- *1 cup raw almonds*
- *1 cup mixed seeds*
- *½ cup sultanas*
- *⅓ cup GF tamari sauce*

Preheat the oven to 180°C. Line a large baking tray with baking paper. In a large bowl, combine the almonds, mixed seeds, and sultanas and drizzle with the tamari. Mix until thoroughly covered. Spread in a single layer on the baking tray. Reserve the extra tamari in the bowl. Bake for 10 minutes. Remove the pan and carefully scrape back into the same bowl (leave the oven on). Toss in the tamari and set aside for 10 minutes. Spread again onto the same baking tray and bake for 5 minutes more. Remove the tray from the oven and let the mixture cool completely. Store at room temperature in an airtight container for up to 3 weeks.

Invite someone special
in your life to share a
soothing cup of tea.

Friends are the family
we choose ourselves.

Raisin Loaf

I first learnt of this recipe at a mothers' group when my second son was just a baby. Mothers' groups are encouraging, supportive, and full of kitchen wisdom!

Serves 8

- *1 tablespoon Nuttelex*
- *1 cup caster sugar*
- *1 cup raisins*
- *1½ cups GF self raising flour*

Position rack in the lower half of the oven and preheat to 180°C. Line a loaf tin with baking paper. In a saucepan, combine the Nuttelex, sugar, raisins, and 1 cup water and bring to a gentle boil. Reduce the heat and simmer for 5 minutes. Set aside to cool. Add the flour and mix well. Turn mixture into prepared tin and bake for 45 minutes.

(WT) *Raisins are good for us—Yippee!!!! In fact, they are considered to be one of the most nutritious dried fruits in the world.*

Lunches

3-Ingredient Pumpkin Soup

My beautiful girlfriend Lisa Darr served this to 20 of us at a dinner party many moons ago … I'll never forget the utter amazement when she told us it was made with just 3 ingredients!

Serves 4 to 6

- *750g pumpkin, peeled and thinly sliced*
- *1.25 litres GF chicken stock*
- *1 large brown onion, sliced*

In a large saucepan, combine all the ingredients. Gently bring to the boil over medium heat, reduce heat, cover and simmer until the pumpkin is tender, 20 to 25 minutes. Blend until smooth.

(WT) *Pumpkins are a storehouse of vitamins and minerals and other healthy nutrients. Pumpkins are rich in vitamin A & C, magnesium (magnesium facilitates the absorption of calcium, helping to maintain our bones and teeth), zinc and fibre. The high amount of fibre helps lower the bad cholesterol (LDL) levels in the blood … The moral of the story is eat more pumpkin!*

Beautiful Burgers

Relished Burgers

Makes 4

- 500g lean beef (or chicken) mince
- ½ cup GF BBQ sauce
- ¼ cup GF gherkin relish
- ½ Spanish onion, finely diced

Combine all the ingredients and shape into four patties. Grill over medium heat for 4 minutes each side, or until browned and cooked through.

Smokey Burgers

Makes 4

- 500g lean beef mince
- 1 red onion, finely diced
- 1 tablespoon smoked paprika
- ½ tablespoon ground cinnamon

In a bowl combine all ingredients. Season with sea salt and cracked pepper. Mix to combine, then shape into four patties and grill 4 minutes each side, or until cooked through.

WT *Serve with a slice of char-grilled pineapple … Delightful!*

Chicken & Corn Soup

Nothing conjures up feelings of home and comfort more than a good flavoursome chicken soup!

Serves 2

- *2 cups GF chicken stock*
- *½ cup cooked rice*
- *1 large egg, beaten*
- *¾ cup (130g) shredded cooked chicken*

In a saucepan, combine the stock and rice then bring to a boil. Add the egg and continue to stir until cooked. Add the shredded chicken and season with cracked pepper. You can thicken this by using less broth and more rice to make it more of a stew.

(WT) *Within me lies a thrifty refusal to throw anything away. As a result I added some spring onion that I had in the fridge for added flavour and texture to this soup!*

Green Curry Chicken Skewers

I was sold at green curry, the rest is just ... clever!

Serves 4

- *500g skinless chicken breast, diced*
- *¼ cup GF green curry paste*
- *1 large red capsicum, cut into 2cm pieces*
- *2 medium zucchini, cut into 2cm pieces*

Place the chicken in a shallow glass or ceramic dish. Add the curry paste and toss to coat. Cover with plastic wrap and refrigerate for at least 20 minutes. Thread the chicken, capsicum, and zucchini onto skewers. Cook for 3 to 4 minutes each side or until the chicken is cooked and the vegetables are tender. Transfer to a plate, cover loosely with foil, and let rest for 5 minutes before serving.

(WT) *Accompany these with a homemade* **Sweet Chilli Sauce**: *In a saucepan, combine 2 tablespoons apple cider vinegar, 3 tablespoons sugar, 200g diced tomatoes and 2 chopped red chillies, seeds removed. Bring to boil over high heat, then reduce the heat and simmer for 7 minutes, stirring occasionally, or until the sauce thickens. Let cool and then puree in a blender or food processor. Pour into a sterilised jar. Secure the lid and refrigerate for up to 3 weeks.*

Mango Salsa

Makes 1

- *Grated zest and juice of ½ lime*
- *½ red capsicum, finely chopped*
- *1 cup mango cubes*
- *3 sprigs coriander, finely chopped*

Combine all the ingredients, season with sea salt and cracked pepper and mix well.

WT *This is a superb accompaniment with any seafood, especially grilled prawns (as pictured). Or try it served with my **Lime-Grilled Chicken**: Mix ½ cup lime juice, ⅓ cup olive oil, 3 tablespoons honey and 1 teaspoon fresh thyme leaves. Season to taste. Marinate chicken for 3 hours then grill for 4 minutes on each side, or until the chicken is cooked through.*

Parsnip 'Rice'

Serves 6

- *2 large parsnips, peeled and grated*
- *1 tablespoon tahini*
- *1 tablespoon soy sauce*
- *2 tablespoons rice vinegar*

In a large bowl, combine all the ingredients and mix well. Cover and let stand for 15 minutes, then with clean hands, massage together to create a rice-like resemblance. Serve over salad, as a side dish to a salmon or tuna ceviche, stuffed into nori rolls, or in lettuce cups, as shown here.

(WT) *Once I learnt the nutritional content of parsnips, I frantically started to search for ways to add it to my family's daily diet. Parsnips are very high in fibre, specifically soluble fibre, which is responsible for lowering cholesterol levels and regulating blood sugar. In addition, their high fibre content makes them an incredible fat-burning food!*

Parsnip Rice Sushi

Serves 6

- *2 nori / seaweed sheets*
- *1½ cups parsnip rice*
- *½ red capsicum, deseeded and diced*
- *1 avocado, peeled and sliced*

Place a nori sheet onto bamboo mat, shiny side down and spread with half the parsnip rice leaving a 1cm border. Line with capsicum and avocado and roll gently but firmly using the bamboo mat (these are cheap to buy and can be found in the Asian section of most supermarkets) to create a compact roll. Remove from the mat, and with a wet knife, cut into 2cm rounds. Chill before serving.

(WT) *For that authentic Japanese flavour serve with GF soy sauce, wasabi and pickled ginger, sensational, fresh and healthy!*

Polenta Cakes

Serves 4

- *2 cups GF vegetable stock*
- *½ cup fine polenta*
- *½ cup grated Parmesan cheese*
- *3 tablespoons Nuttelex*

In a saucepan, bring the stock to a boil and stir in the polenta. Continue stirring, until the mixture has thickened and is creamy. Add the Parmesan and 2 tablespoons of the Nuttelex and mix well. Season with sea salt and pepper. Spoon the polenta into a greased 20cm round cake tin and refrigerate until completely cold. To serve, cut into 8 wedges. In a frying pan, heat the remaining 1 tablespoon Nuttelex and fry the polenta wedges until crisp and golden on both sides. Alternatively, divide the mixture across 4 greased egg rings and lightly fry.

WT *Add any number of fresh and healthy herbs and veggies to these fabulous little cakes. Serve with a dollop of olive tapenade or sun dried tomato pesto – super duper!*

Salmon & Corn Petit-Pies

One of the joys of this recipe is how quick and easy they are to make — another is how popular they are when served ☺

Makes 24

- *4 eggs*
- *1 can (220g) salmon, drained and flaked*
- *2 ears of corn, husked and kernels removed*
- *2 tablespoons chopped fresh chives*

Preheat the oven to 180°C. In a large bowl, whisk the eggs. Add the salmon, corn and chives. Season to taste and mix well. Pour into 2 x 12 cup silicone mini-muffin trays. Bake until golden and set, about 15 to 20 minutes.

(WT) *For an inspired finish, mix a little lemon zest into natural LF yoghurt and season. Dollop onto each little pie and stud with a basil leaf or flower, lavender leaf or flower or a combination of both.*

Sizzling Beef Bites

Makes 24

- *250g beef minute steak, quartered*
- *1 bunch spring onions, cut into 3 to 4cm lengths*
- *½ cup GF teriyaki sauce*
- *1 tablespoon sesame oil*

Onto each beef strip, place a piece of spring onion and roll to enclose. Secure with a toothpick or small bamboo skewer. Brush each skewer liberally with some of the teriyaki sauce (reserve the remaining sauce). Heat the sesame oil in a nonstick frying pan over high heat. Working in batches, fry the skewers for 2 to 3 minutes, turning and basting until done to your liking. When done, set aside and cover with foil. Add the reserved teriyaki sauce to the pan and simmer for 2 to 3 minutes or until slightly reduced. Serve drizzled over the beef bites and season to taste.

Salads, Sauces
& Dressings

It's easy to turn the simplest salads and mains into flavourful masterpieces with delicious dressings and sauces.

Here is a selection of some of my favourites.

Avocado, Mango & Bacon Salad

Delight in the 'oohs' and 'aahs' this dish elicits when served.

Serves 4

- *2 mangoes*
- *2 avocados*
- *8 slices GF bacon, rind removed, cut and cooked*

Thinly slice the mango and avocado. Place a timbale (a cylindrical, hollow mould) in the middle of a serving plate and into its base alternate layers, starting with avocado, then mango, then bacon. Continue to stack, finishing with a few pieces of yummy crispy bacon. Place two fingers on the top of the stack, press down the contents within, then gently remove the timbale. Serve with a simple salad to compliment.

Homemade Dressings

Classic Vinaigrette

Makes 1 cup

- ½ cup (125ml) fresh lemon juice
- 4 tablespoons extra-virgin olive oil
- 2 teaspoons GF Dijon mustard
- 2 cloves garlic, crushed

In a screw-top jar, combine all the ingredients and season with sea salt and cracked pepper to taste. Shake well and then drizzle over green salads, garden salads and a divine mix of basil leaves, lentils, cherry tomatoes and Spanish onions (finely sliced).

Sweet Chilli Dressing

Makes ½ cup

- 3 tablespoons sweet chilli sauce
- 3 tablespoons fresh lime juice
- ½ teaspoon chopped fresh ginger
- ¼ (60ml) cup vegetable oil

In a bowl, stir together the chilli sauce, lime juice and ginger. Whisk in the oil. Add some toasted sesame seeds.

WT *For a delicious, homemade **Caramelised Balsamic Vinegar** see page 80.*

Homemade Sauces

Condiments aren't just toppings, they are food, choose them wisely …

BBQ Sauce

Makes ½ cup

- *1 clove garlic, minced*
- *1 tablespoon brown sugar*
- *1 tablespoon cider vinegar*
- *¼ cup tomato paste*

In a small bowl, combine all the ingredients and season with sea salt and pepper to taste.

Tomato Sauce

Makes ½ cup

- *¼ cup extra-virgin olive oil*
- *¼ cup raw honey*
- *2 tablespoons fresh lemon juice*
- *2 cups sun-dried tomatoes*

In a blender, combine the olive oil, honey, lemon juice and 1 teaspoon sea salt. Blend until well combined. Add the sun-dried tomatoes and continue blending until a thick paste forms. Store in the refrigerator for up to 14 days.

Pear, Parmesan & Beetroot

This is the perfect salad. It has vibrant colours and a slightly sweet taste with a lemony kick. It is raw and robust.

Serves 4

- *2 beetroots, peeled*
- *2 ripe pears, thinly sliced*
- *30g shaved Parmesan cheese*
- *Juice of ½ lemon*

Using gloves to protect your hands, grate the beets (or if you have a spiralizer, use that to spiralize the pears first, then the beets). Simply arrange the pears, beets, and Parmesan in a serving bowl. Drizzle with the lemon juice, season with sea salt and pepper, and lightly toss. Be careful when tossing, as the beets will turn everything purple (or a pretty shade of pink)!

(WT) *Apart from having no fat and very few calories, the high volume of soluble fibre found in beetroot also feeds good bacteria in our gut, helping to lower our cholesterol levels, keeping us happy and healthy.*

When buying strawberries, always search
for those reddest toward the hull, they
will be naturally sweeter.

Strawberry & Kale

Serves 4 to 6

- *200g kale, stems removed, coarsely chopped*
- *250g strawberries, sliced*
- *¾ cup sunflower seeds*

Add the kale leaves to a large salad bowl. Sprinkle with strawberries and sunflower seeds. Toss gently then drizzle with this yummy dressing.

Caramelised Balsamic Vinegar

- *⅓ cup (83ml) balsamic vinegar*
- *⅔ cup (166ml) extra-virgin olive oil*
- *2 teaspoons caster sugar*
- *1 tablespoon finely chopped fresh chives*

In a screw-top jar, combine the vinegar, oil, sugar, chives, 1 tablespoon water and salt and pepper to taste. Shake really, really well. Taste and adjust seasonings, if required.

WT *Include kale in your diet, and you'll add a great source of antioxidants, fibre, and so much more. The 'Queen of Greens,' Kale is low in calorie, high in fibre, and has zero fat.*

Mains

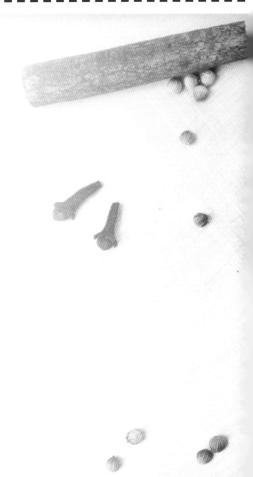

Baked Garlic Chicken

Serves 4

- 6 garlic cloves, minced
- 2 tablespoons olive oil
- 1 cup brown sugar
- 4 boneless, skinless chicken breast halves

Preheat the oven to 200°C. Lightly grease a baking dish. In small frying pan, sauté the garlic in the oil until tender, about 30 seconds. Remove from the heat and stir in the brown sugar. Place the chicken breasts in the baking dish and cover with the garlic and brown sugar mixture. Season with salt and pepper to taste. Bake uncovered for 15 to 20 minutes.

WT *For a beautiful **Balsamic-Glazed Chicken**: Roast two chicken breasts seasoned with sea salt and cracked pepper in a 180°C oven for 6 minutes. In a small saucepan, heat ¼ cup strawberry jam, 2 tablespoons balsamic vinegar, and ½ teaspoon dried thyme over low heat until the jam melts. Brush liberally with the glaze and roast, brushing twice more, for 8 to 10 minutes or until the chicken is golden glazed and cooked through.*

Carbonara Sauce

I will never make Carbonara Sauce any other way!

Makes about 1½ cups

- *2 tablespoons pure maize cornflour*
- *2 cups almond milk*
- *1 teaspoon tamari soy sauce*
- *2 teaspoons GF vegetable stock*

Stir the cornflour into one-quarter cup of the almond milk until nice and smooth. Pour the mixture into a saucepan and add the remaining ingredients. Cook, stirring constantly, over medium / low heat until thickened and warmed through. Season with sea salt and cracked pepper and serve over your favourite pasta.

WT *Totally make this your own by adding to it whatever you like; mushrooms, garlic, onion or GF bacon. With a growing range of calcium-rich, dairy alternatives available in supermarkets, going dairy-free no longer means missing out. Soy milk is one of the more popular, or for those of you with a soy intolerance try almond milk, rice milk or oat milk.*

Chilli Crab Cakes

These are a sure way to whip up a quick dinner to impress your family and friends.

Makes 5

- *4 ears of corn, husked*
- *4 eggs*
- *250g crabmeat, fresh or tinned*
- *2 long chillies, seeded and finely chopped*

In a saucepan of boiling water, cook the corn until tender, about 5 minutes. Remove the kernels from the corn and pulse in a blender until just crushed. Whisk the eggs and combine with the crab, chillies, and corn kernels. Season with sea salt and cracked black pepper. Heat a large nonstick frying pan over medium / high heat and fry the batter in 10cm fritter rounds, turning once when golden.

(WT) *Serve these delicious cakes stacked with fresh, crisp salad or creamy, seasonal slices of avocado.*

Citrus Candied Salmon

This is just heavenly.

Serves 2

- *⅓ cup brown sugar*
- *Grated zest of 1 lemon*
- *2 salmon steaks*
- *1 tablespoon olive oil*

In a small bowl, mix together the brown sugar, lemon zest, 1 teaspoon sea salt, and ½ teaspoon cracked black pepper. Rub the salmon steaks with the oil. Heat a nonstick frying pan over medium heat, add the salmon, and cook for 2 minutes each side, then transfer to a paper-lined baking tray, skin side up, and spread with the brown sugar mixture. Grill for 2 to 3 minutes or until the sugar caramelises. Let stand for a few minutes before serving.

(WT) *Salmon is a nutritional powerhouse, so for another culinary sensation try this delectable* **Wasabi Salmon**: *Combine 2 teaspoons wasabi paste, ¼ cup tamari sauce, and ½ teaspoon sesame oil in a bowl. Add the salmon, turn several times, and marinate for 20 minutes. Grill to your liking.*

Coffee & Pepper Crusted Steak

This is charmingly unusual, and one I love due to its flavour and absolute ease.

Serves 4

- *4 steaks, 2 to 3cm thick*
- *2 tablespoons olive oil*
- *2 tablespoons whole coffee beans*
- *2 tablespoons whole black peppercorns*

Rub each steak with oil. Coarsely grind the coffee beans and peppercorns, and then press the mixture onto both sides of the steaks. Grill or barbecue the steaks over high heat for 3 to 4 minutes each side. Turn only when beads of juice appear on the steak's surface. Remove from the grill and season both sides with sea salt. Allow to rest for 3 minutes before serving.

Lovely LAKSA

Serves 2

- *2 tablespoons GF Thai laksa paste*
- *1 chicken breast, cut into chunks*
- *1 can (440g) coconut milk*
- *100g GF vermicelli*

In a saucepan, combine the laksa paste and 1 tablespoon water and stir over medium heat to release the flavour of the laksa. Add the chicken and cook, stirring, for 1 to 2 minutes. Add the coconut milk and half a cup of water, gently bring to a boil, then reduce the heat and simmer for 7 minutes. Meanwhile, in a large bowl, empty the vermicelli into a bowl and cover with boiling water. Sit for 5 minutes so the noodles soften. Use a fork to stir and separate. Strain and add to the chicken laksa. Stir to coat.

(WT) *Add whatever veggies you and your family will eat to this richly flavoured dish. Garnish with sliced spring onions and chillies to serve.*

Lamb Cutlets Kilpatrick

My beautiful 10-year-old boy would ask for this every single week at least once …
It is his belief that food is just better with bacon in it ☺

Serves 4

- *16 lamb cutlets*
- *6 slices GF bacon, chopped*
- *½ cup GF BBQ sauce*

In a large frying pan, cook the cutlets over high heat, 2 to 3 minutes each side or until done to your liking. Place on a paper-lined baking tray and let rest. Meanwhile, preheat the grill. To the same pan, add the chopped bacon and sauté until just cooked. Add the BBQ sauce and stir. Season to taste. Top each cutlet with the sticky bacon mixture and grill for 1 to 2 minutes or until nice and crispy.

WT *Lamb (in fact all meats) are a fantastic source of protein, containing 9 essential amino acids. It is an especially good source of easily absorbed zinc and iron.*

Minty Lamb Rissoles

Serves 4

- *500g minced lamb*
- *½ cup sultanas*
- *2 teaspoons GF curry powder*
- *8 chopped fresh mint leaves*

In a large bowl, mix all the ingredients together and season with sea salt and cracked pepper. Roll into 8 evenly sized balls and cook in a nonstick frying pan over medium heat for 4 minutes on each side or until cooked through and quite crunchy on the outside.

(WT) *These are lovely served in a GF wrap, with salad and hummus. If your children aren't partial to curry, simply substitute dried apricots for the curry powder and roll the balls smaller for yummy* **Lamb and Apricot Meatballs**! *Herbs are best picked just before they come into flower and early in the morning before the sun gets too strong, but not after it has rained.*

Food is first eaten with the eyes; a simple meal can be easily transformed into a 'visual feast' by adding some bright and vibrant edible flowers.

Mustard & Thyme Chicken Breast

Serves 2

- *2 boneless, skinless chicken breast halves*
- *¼ cup raw honey*
- *¼ bunch fresh lemon thyme*
- *2 tablespoons GF wholegrain mustard*

Preheat the oven to 180°C. Line a baking tray with baking paper. Butterfly or flatten the chicken breasts. Spread with honey and mustard. Place the thyme sprigs in the middle of the breast allowing some of the leaves to hang over one end. Roll up and secure with kitchen twine or toothpicks. Place on the baking tray, season with sea salt and pepper, and bake for 20 minutes, basting halfway through.

(WT) *This easy dish has many strings to its bow: It is incredibly versatile. It is an easy midweek dinner, a great entertainer, and it often envelopes many a leftover. Mix and match using antipasto: GF basil pesto, GF prosciutto, artichoke hearts, or marinated capsicums.*

Shepherd's Pie

Serves 6

- *500g lean mince*
- *½ cup GF fruit chutney*
- *400g cauliflower*
- *1 tablespoon olive oil*

Preheat the oven to 180°C. In a nonstick frying pan, brown the mince over medium heat. Season with sea salt and pepper and mix the chutney through. Reduce the heat and simmer for 10 minutes. Meanwhile, remove the florets from the cauliflower. Cook the florets in a saucepan of gently boiling water until tender, 4 to 6 minutes. Drain, add the olive oil, sea salt and pepper, and mash until nice and smooth. Pour the mince into a baking dish, top with an even layer of mashed cauliflower, and season again lightly. Bake until the top is golden around the rim, about 15 minutes.

(WT) *Pureed or mashed cauliflower is a fantastic substitute for mashed potatoes. Low in carbohydrates and high in nutrients and the taste ~ well it's what makes it!*

Spanish Tortilla

Serves 4

- ¼ cup olive oil
- 3 medium potatoes (600g), thinly sliced
- 1 brown onion, diced
- 6 eggs, lightly beaten

Preheat the oven to 180°C. In a large nonstick frying pan, heat the oil over medium / high heat. Add the potatoes and onion, cover, and cook, stirring occasionally, until golden and tender. Add the eggs to the pan and season with sea salt and pepper. Reduce the heat and cook, uncovered, until the egg is just set, about 5 minutes. Place the pan in the oven and grill for 4 minutes or until golden brown. Loosen gently with a spatula and carefully slide the tortilla onto a large plate, then cut into wedges to serve. Serve as is or with this healthy Corn Salsa …

Corn Salsa

Makes about 2 cups

- 2 ears of corn, husked
- 1 red onion, finely diced
- ½ red capsicum, finely chopped
- 1 tablespoon fresh lemon juice

In a saucepan of boiling salted water, cook the corn for 5 minutes or until tender. Let cool slightly, then cut the kernels from the cob. In a medium bowl, combine the corn, onion, capsicum and lemon juice. Taste and season with sea salt and pepper.

Thai Chickpea Patties

These are fabulous used as vegetable burgers, or served atop crisp, thin apple slices, with a dollop of hummus and topped with half a cherry tomato.

Makes 12

- *500g sweet potato, peeled and cut into 3cm cubes*
- *2 cans (400g each) chickpeas, drained*
- *½ cup finely chopped spring onion*
- *¼ cup GF red curry paste*

Preheat the oven to 180°C. Line a baking tray with baking paper. Place the sweet potato on a microwave-safe plate in a single layer. Cover and microwave on high for 3 to 4 minutes or until just tender. Drain and transfer to a large bowl. Add the chickpeas and mash until almost smooth. Stir in the spring onion and curry paste and season to taste with sea salt and cracked pepper. Mix until well combined. Using damp hands, form the mixture into 12 patties and place on the baking tray. Bake for 20 minutes.

(WT) *Chickpeas really are the world's food. They are known as Garbanzos in Spanish speaking countries, Pois Chiches in France, Chana in India, and Hummus in Israel and Arabic countries. I love them not only because they taste good, but because they are so very good for us!*

Tropical Pork Satay Sticks

Serves 4

- ¾ cup (185ml) coconut milk
- 2 tablespoons crunchy peanut butter
- 2 teaspoons GF curry powder
- 2 pork chops, trimmed and cut into 2cm cubes

In a medium bowl, mix together the coconut milk, peanut butter, curry powder, and sea salt and pepper to taste until well combined. Add the pork, stir to coat, and marinate in the refrigerator for at least 1 hour. Soak 12 bamboo skewers in water before threading with the pork. Cook on a hot grill, turning constantly so as not to burn. Continue to glaze throughout.

(WT) *Alternate pork with cubes of unpeeled apple, pear or nashi as I did the day of the photo shoot.*

Tuna & Tomato Risotto

Serves 4

- *1.25 litres GF vegetable stock*
- *2 cups Arborio rice*
- *425g can flaked tuna in springwater, drained*
- *1 cup freshly chopped tomatoes*

In a large saucepan, bring the stock to a boil, add the rice and stir. Reduce the heat, cover and simmer for 15 minutes. Add the tuna and tomatoes, season with sea salt and pepper. Continue to simmer, stirring regularly, until all the liquid has been absorbed. Serve immediately.

(WT) *A serving of 100g of tuna in spring water has roughly 100 calories, while tuna in oil has nearly double the amount with 190 … Keep it in mind next time you are faced with the option!*

Desserts

Avocado & Coconut Ice Cream

Serves 6

- *3 avocados*
- *1 can (400ml) coconut milk*
- *2 tablespoons agave nectar*
- *12 fresh cherries*

Scoop the avocado pulp out, cut into chunks, and place in a blender or food processor. Add the coconut milk and nectar, and puree until smooth. Pour into a paper-lined loaf tin and place in the freezer for 1 hour. Remove and blend again. Pour back into the loaf tin and freeze for 3 to 4 hours or until set. Serve on a long, rectangular platter garnished with the cherries.

WT *Creamy rich avocado is considered the world's healthiest fruit because of its nutrient content, such as vitamin K, fibre, potassium, folate, vitamin B6, vitamin C and copper.*

Beautiful Banana Ice Cream

How can 1 simple ingredient make such a remarkable dessert?

Serves 4

- *4 ripe bananas, chopped*

Freeze the bananas. Place half in a blender with 2 tablespoons water. Blend for 30 seconds, then scrape down the sides. Add half of the remaining bananas and blend for another 30 seconds. Again, scrape down the sides before adding the final amount. Blend now for 1 to 2 minutes or until the bananas turn into a rich, creamy ice cream.

Cacao & Date Truffles

Makes 16

- *3 tablespoons raw cacao powder*
- *1½ cups Medjool dates, pitted*
- *3 tablespoons shredded coconut*
- *½ cup pistachios, lightly toasted and crushed*

Blend together the cacao, dates and coconut. Roll into balls and then into the crushed pistachios to coat. Chill before serving.

(WT) *Another beautiful variation are my **Key Lime Balls**: Simply blend ½ cup Medjool dates, ¼ cup almonds, 1 tablespoon lime juice, 1 teaspoon grated lime zest, and 3 tablespoons shredded coconut. (I do these regularly in my Thermochef, but a good sturdy food processor would work too.) Roll, chill, and enjoy!*

Cheesecake Base

Makes 1 base (or 4 smaller ones)

- *2 cups (240g) raw, unsalted almonds*
- *12 fresh Medjool dates, pitted*
- *½ cup shredded coconut*

Place all the ingredients into a food processor and blend until quite fine and well combined. You may need to stop and use a spatula to scrape the mixture down onto the blades. Scrape the mixture into a baking paper lined, 20cm cake tin, press it into the corners of the base and up the sides and chill for at least 1 hour before filling.

WT *I made the **Avocado & Coconut Ice Cream** on page 118 as a filling. Simply cut desired quantity into chunks and blend until nice and smooth. Spoon or pipe into the cheesecake base. Same with the **Chocolate Mousse**, page 128, it also makes a beautiful 'Chocolate Cheesecake' combined with this base.*

Caramel Pavlova

Serves 4 to 6

- *6 egg whites*
- *1½ cups (300g) firmly packed brown sugar*
- *2 teaspoons white vinegar*
- *1 tablespoon pure maize cornflour, sifted*

Preheat the oven to 200°C. Line a large baking tray with baking paper. Place the egg whites, brown sugar, and vinegar in a large bowl of an electric mixer. Beat on high speed for 10 to 12 minutes or until stiff peaks form. Using a whisk, fold in the sifted cornflour. Spoon the mixture, either as one large mound or into four smaller ones. Place in the oven and immediately reduce the temperature to 100°C. If in one large mound, bake for 2 to 2½ hours or until the Pavlova is dry to the touch. If four smaller ones, bake for 1 to 1½ hours. Turn off the oven, set the door ajar, and let the Pavlova(s) cool completely.

WT *The brown sugar gives a delicious caramel flavour, and the addition of pure maize cornflour and vinegar results in a crispy exterior, marshmallow-like interior.*

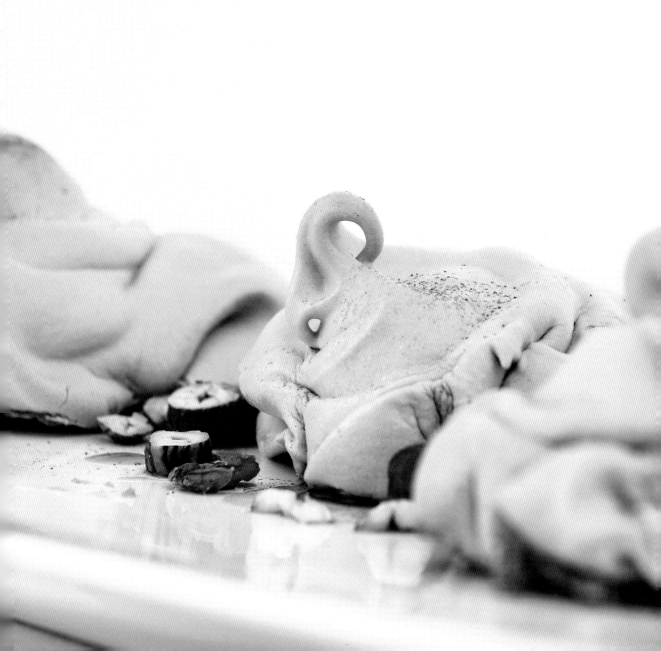

Chocolate Mousse

A healthy twist on a traditional favourite that will have you and your guests enthralled!

Serves 2

- *2 avocados*
- *1 banana*
- *1 cup raw cacao powder*
- *½ cup pure maple syrup*

Scoop the pulp of the avocados into a food processor, add the banana, cacao, and maple syrup and blend until smooth. Pipe or spoon into glasses … *Enjoy!*

WT *For a visual delight, decorate with bright edible petals and fresh seasonal berries.*

Chocolate, Quinoa & Pecan Mud Cake

I was so impressed with this cake, it has become my 'go-to' cake for all occasions.

Serves 8

- *2 cups quinoa, rinsed*
- *3 eggs, separated*
- *1 cup pecans, coarsely chopped*
- *200g dark LF chocolate, melted*

Preheat the oven to 180°C. Line 2 x 20cm greaseproof cake tins with baking paper. In a saucepan, combine the quinoa and 3 cups of water. Bring to a boil, stir, then cover and reduce to a simmer. Cook for 15 minutes. Remove the quinoa from the heat and allow to sit for 5 minutes with the lid on. Meanwhile, in a large bowl, whisk the egg whites to soft peaks. In a separate bowl, combine the quinoa, egg yolks and pecans, and mix well. Add the melted chocolate, and then gently fold through the egg whites. Pour into the prepared cake pans and bake for 30 minutes.

WT *Also delicious with dates instead of pecans and served sandwiched together with extra melted chocolate.*

Coconut Panna Cotta

Serves 2

- *2 tablespoons raw honey*
- *10g sachet gelatine*
- *½ cup caster sugar*
- *1 can (400g) coconut milk*

In a saucepan, stir together the honey, gelatine, sugar, and coconut milk. Bring to a gentle boil over medium heat, stirring for 3 minutes to dissolve the sugar and gelatine. Divide the mixture evenly between 2 (or 3 smaller) serving glasses or dishes. Cool to room temperature. Cover and refrigerate for at least 4 hours to set.

(WT) *Often Panna Cotta is served with chocolate curls for a contrast of colour, but try these super easy **Candied Grapes**. Simply roll the grapes into caster sugar and let sit for an hour to set.*

Strawberry Boats with Coconut Whipped Cream

There's nothing finer that the discovery of a simple dessert that is soooo popular ~ this is the one!

Serves 6 to 8

- *1 can (270ml) premium coconut cream*
- *1 teaspoon agave nectar (or more to taste)*
- *250g strawberries*

Chill the coconut cream overnight in the refrigerator. Open and drain off the clear liquid, transfer the cream to a chilled bowl, using a knife to scrape all the cream out of the can. Using an electric mixer, beat the cream and agave nectar until thick and fluffy. Slice the strawberries in half and pipe the coconut cream onto them. **Chocolate Mousse** (page 128) also marries beautifully with fresh, seasonal strawberries.

WT *For flavoured coconut whipped cream, add some cinnamon, instant coffee or raw cocao powder.*

Sticky Mango Rice

This is a fabulously comforting dessert, but then again, aren't all rice puddings?

Serves 6

- *1 cup short-grain rice*
- *¼ cup sugar*
- *1 can (270ml) coconut cream*
- *3 mangoes, sliced*

In a saucepan, combine the rice and 1½ cups water. Bring to a boil, reduce the heat, cover, and cook for about 10 minutes. Add the sugar and 1 cup (250ml) of the coconut cream (reserve a little for garnish), stirring until combined and nice and soft. Dollop the mixture into serving bowls and serve with freshly sliced mango and drizzled with the remaining coconut cream.

WT *When mangoes are in season and plentiful, puree the flesh of one for a delicious* **'Mango Couli'**. *Spoon 2 tablespoons into the bowl, before topping with the yummy rice. This couli freezes beautifully and can be used at a later date in muffin and cake batters, smoothies and juices.*

ThankYou

One man can be a crucial
ingredient on a team,
but he cannot make a team!

Kareem Abdul-Jabbor

Reach Out
Join our Foodie Family

At 4 Ingredients we cultivate a family of busy people all bound together by the desire to create good, healthy, homemade meals quickly, easily and economically.

Our aim is to save us all precious time and money in the kitchen. If this is you too, then we invite you to join our growing family where we share kitchen wisdom daily.

If you have a favourite recipe, or a tip that has worked for you in your kitchen and think others would enjoy it, please join our family at:

facebook.com/4ingredientspage

@4ingredients

4 Ingredients Channel

4ingredients.com.au

@4ingredients

With Love
Kim

Index

Bibliography

Websites

For an incredible amount of useful information and research:
www.coeliac.org.au

Not only lists gluten free foods but where you get them and brands:
www.glutenfreeandeasy.com

The largest collection of gluten free recipes in the world:
www.glutenfreeda.com

What is coeliac disease:
www.coeliac.org.au/coeliac-disease

Everything you need to know about food. Know what you eat:
www.nutritiondata.self.com

Books Magazines & Journals

Cattassi. C. et al. *When is a coeliac a coeliac?* European Journal of Gastroenterology and Hepatology. 2001 13(9): 1123-8.

McCosker, Kim and Bermingham, Rachael. *4 Ingredients Gluten Free*. 4 Ingredients, PO Box 400 Caloundra Queensland 4551 Australia, 2008.

McCosker, Kim, Bermingham, Rachael and Chopra, Deepak. *4 Ingredients Fast, Fresh & Healthy*. 4 Ingredients, PO Box 400 Caloundra Queensland 4551 Australia, 2009.

Korn, Donna and Clough, Margaret. *Gluten Free for Dummies*. John Wiley and Sons, 42 McDougall Street, Milton, Queensland 4064 Australia, 2008.